Machines at work

TRUCK

LONDON, NEW YORK, MUNICH,
MELBOURNE, and DELHI

Written and edited by Elizabeth Haldane
Designed by Mary Sandberg

Publishing manager Susan Leonard
Managing art editor Clare Shedden
Jacket design Neal Coburne
Picture researcher Anna Bedewell
Production Emma Hughes
DTP Designer Almudena Díaz
Consultant Dave Young

Published in the United States by
DK Publishing, Inc.
375 Hudson Street
New York, New York 10014

05 06 07 08 09   10 9 8 7 6 5 4 3 2 1

A Cataloging-in-Publication record for this book
is available from the Library of Congress.

ISBN 0-7566-1142-3

Color reproduction by GRB Editrice, S.r.l., Verona, Italy
Printed and bound in China by Toppan Printing Co., Ltd.

Discover more at
www.dk.com

Contents

Get trucking!

Trucks come in many different shapes and sizes. The largest ones come in two parts that can be hooked together. The front part is called a **tractor unit** and the back part is called a **trailer**.

In one piece
Some trucks have a body but not a trailer. They are called rigid trucks and cannot bend around corners.

This axle lifts off the ground when the trailer is empty.

The trailer hooks on to a swiveling device called the "fifth wheel."

Get connected
The driver backs the tractor unit to meet the trailer. He attaches tubes and wires containing air and electricity to the trailer so the rear brakes and lights work.

Bend it
An articulated truck can bend between the tractor and the trailer. This tipping trailer has just dumped its load.

The engine is beneath the driver's cab.

Get loading!

Trucks rule the road, carrying all kinds of **goods** from place to place. They **pick up** their loads at a warehouse, seaport, or airport and **deliver** door-to-door.

Express delivery
Pallets of vegetables are loaded into the back of a box-body truck. They need to get to the supermarket or factory quickly to keep them fresh.

Lots of boxes fit on board.

This type of trailer is called a curtainsider because it has curtains that can be drawn back along the sides.

Buckles secure the curtain.

A forklift truck picks up boxes.

A bigger load

These tree trunks are held in the huge claws of a crane as they are loaded onto a truck. Hauling logs is one of the most dangerous of all trucking operations.

Steel claw

This tractor unit has a big hood. The hood flips forward to reveal the engine.

Fuel tank

Splish, splosh

Tankers carry liquids, powders, and gases in special types of **trailers.** A fuel tanker **delivers** fuel to filling stations. It has special compartments inside the trailer to stop the liquid fuel from sloshing around too much.

Warning sign to show that the tanker is carrying a liquid that can catch fire.

Hazard warning signs

 Fuel tankers carry this warning sign.

 Tankers containing strong chemicals carry this sign.

 Tankers with poisonous gas inside have this sign.

All in a row

A convoy of tankers carries chemicals on a mountain road. Drivers need special training to drive with dangerous chemicals, and safety rules have to be followed.

Fuel is stored in underground storage tanks.

From tanker to tank

The driver attaches a hose to a valve. Different compartments in the tanker have different valves. When the valve is open, the tanker can load or unload.

Dump it down

Giant dump trucks work in **mines** and **quarries**. They carry and dump enormous loads of dirt and rocks twenty-four hours a day, seven days a week.

The body is made of thick steel so that it can carry very heavy loads.

Off-road monster

This giant dump truck is much too big to travel on an ordinary road. When it moves to a new site, it has to be taken apart and carried on a special transporter.

Loading up

At a copper mine, an excavator empties a load into a dump truck. The bucket drops about 50 tons of rock and dirt—that's as heavy as nine elephants.

Clouds of dust fill the air.

Each giant tire costs as much as a new car.

A metal canopy protects the driver from falling rocks.

797B

237

11

Snow shifters

In winter in places where snow falls, trucks called **snowplows** and **snowblowers** go out to work. They clear the roads so other traffic can move.

Snow cloud
The snowblower works by churning the snow up with a spinning drum. As the drum spins, the snow is pushed upward. It then blows out to the other side of the road in a big plume.

Plows in convoy
Sudden daytime blizzards can block roads very quickly, and a whole line of snow plows may be sent to clear the snow.

Snow shoots out...

The blades of
the drum churn
up the snow.

Logs on wheels

Logging trucks carry huge tree trunks. They need **powerful** engines and brakes to carry such a heavy load. The driver has to brake a lot when going downhill out of forest areas.

Grab and go!
A large crane lifts a pile of heavy tree trunks. The grab grips them with its steel claws and loads them carefully onto the truck. Some logging trucks have built-in cranes.

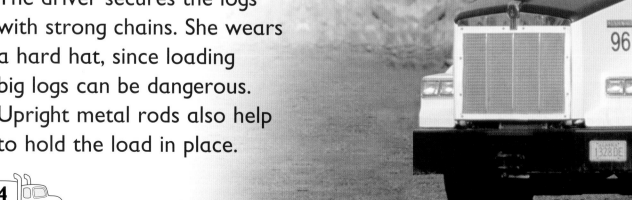

A chrome chimney lets out the exhaust from the engine.

All chained in
The driver secures the logs with strong chains. She wears a hard hat, since loading big logs can be dangerous. Upright metal rods also help to hold the load in place.

Ready for the sawmill
A separate crane loads these logs at a snowy tree-felling site. The logging truck will take them to a sawmill, where they will be stripped of bark and cut up.

15

Trains of the road

The **longest** trucks in the world are called road trains because they pull up to four trailers. They are used in Australia, where distances between cities are **vast**.

Train or truck?
Four road trains are stopped by floods. They are not as long as trains, but they are too big to enter cities.

Beating a dusty trail

Conditions can be harsh in the middle of Australia. This road train thunders past in a cloud of dust. It carries enough fuel to travel about 2,200 miles (3,500 km).

Up to 400 head of cattle can be carried.

Roo crossing!

In the Australian bush (open country), wandering kangaroos can cause a lot of damage if they hit a moving road train. That's why road trains have metal "roo" bars.

ROAD TRAIN

NEXT 5km

Car carrier

With its special trailer, this **car transporter** can carry ten cars from a factory to a car **showroom**. It takes about an hour to load all the cars.

Each car is driven onto a separate deck, which is then raised.

A precious load

Driving this truck is a big responsibility. The driver needs skill and special training. He has to be careful to load and attach the cars safely.

This car transporter can carry 10 cars.

Formula 1

Race cars are carried to race tracks in specially designed trucks. A platform moved by remote control lifts each car into and out of the transporter.

Ladder for reaching the top car to tie it in.

Works of art!

Customized trucks have **special** features that make them stand out from other trucks. They may have lots of **shiny** metal parts, hand-painted decoration, and even a luxurious interior. Many of them compete in truck shows.

American beauty
Eye-catching decoration is a great advertisement for the truck and its owner. Prizes are awarded for customized trucks at the major truck shows.

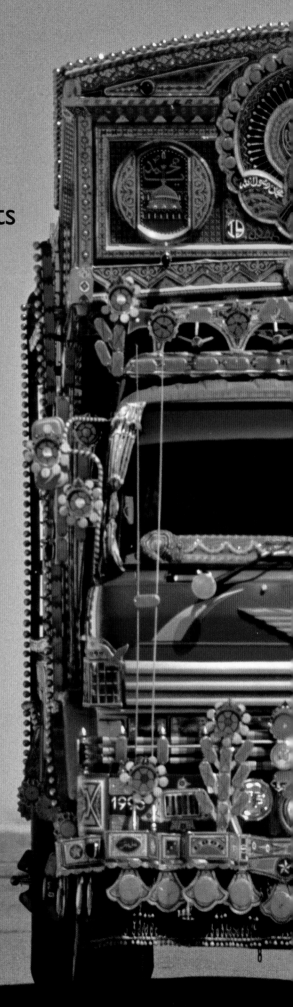

Golden truck

Brightly colored flowers and religious symbols decorate this Asian truck. Drivers of such trucks believe the holy images will protect them when on the road.

This golden truck can be seen from far away.

Extra lights and horns

Painted prize-winner

The amazing pictures on this working truck were done by an airbrush artist. Inside the cab, the seats are covered with cream-colored leather. This truck has won prizes at truck shows.

The need for speed

A dragster truck roars along the track, reaching 256 mph (412 k/mh) in 6.36 seconds. It has a jet engine taken from a **fighter** plane and is specially built for **speed**.

Is it a record?
Jet trucks do not race against each other but try to beat speed records on their own.

Great balls of fire...

Up, up, and away
A customized tractor unit does wheelies. A heavy weight in the rear of the truck helps the front to rise up.

It's a fact

🚚 Race trucks are very noisy. Most tracks have rules to say that trucks should be quieter than thunder!

🚚 Some race trucks have the same power as 1,300 horses.

🚚 Over the same distance, race trucks use four times as much diesel as an average truck.

The race is on!

Truck racing is a popular sport and different kinds of trucks take part, from pickup trucks to articulated tractor units like these.

Into the future

Truck manufacturers build concept trucks to **experiment** with new ideas. They want to find ways of allowing air to move more easily around the body of a truck so that it slows the truck less.

The rounded shape of the cab creates less resistance to wind.

An engineer releases the special fog.

A never-ending experiment

In a wind tunnel, an engineer uses a special fog to see how air flows around windows and mirrors as well as over and under the truck. The more easily the truck moves through the air, the less fuel it uses.

Shape of the future?

Big trucks have to push against a lot of air as they move on the road. This concept truck has a wedge-shaped cab that slips through the air with less resistance than a standard-shape cab.

Driver's cab

A new generation

This streamlined truck was designed by Renault. Instead of rear-view mirrors, it has cameras that send images to monitors in the driver's cab.

Monster machines

Some of the biggest wheels in this book belong to **monster trucks**. These amazing stunt vehicles started out as **sideshows** at car fairs.

Watch my flags fly as I go by.

Owners name their trucks and decorate them with bright colors.

That's wheely big!

The huge wheels on monster trucks can be many times the size of the tires on a family car. Four children can stand inside the wheel hub of Bigfoot 5, one of the best-known monster trucks.

I'll race you!

Monster racing can be dangerous. Driving fast can make the truck roll over. The trucks have to weigh 5 tons for safety. That's five times the weight of an ordinary car.

The trucks have bright headlights for events at night.

We have liftoff

The monster truck has four-wheel drive and a very powerful engine. This helps it to jump and fly through the air over a row of cars.

Deep treads give a good grip in mud.

Days of old

The first trucks were nothing like those of today. They were **powered** by steam, had **solid** tires, and often got bogged down in mud and sand.

This tanker was loaded from the top.

Vintage logger, 1929
When empty, this early logging truck carried part of the trailer to reduce its overall length. The driver got little protection from the cold.

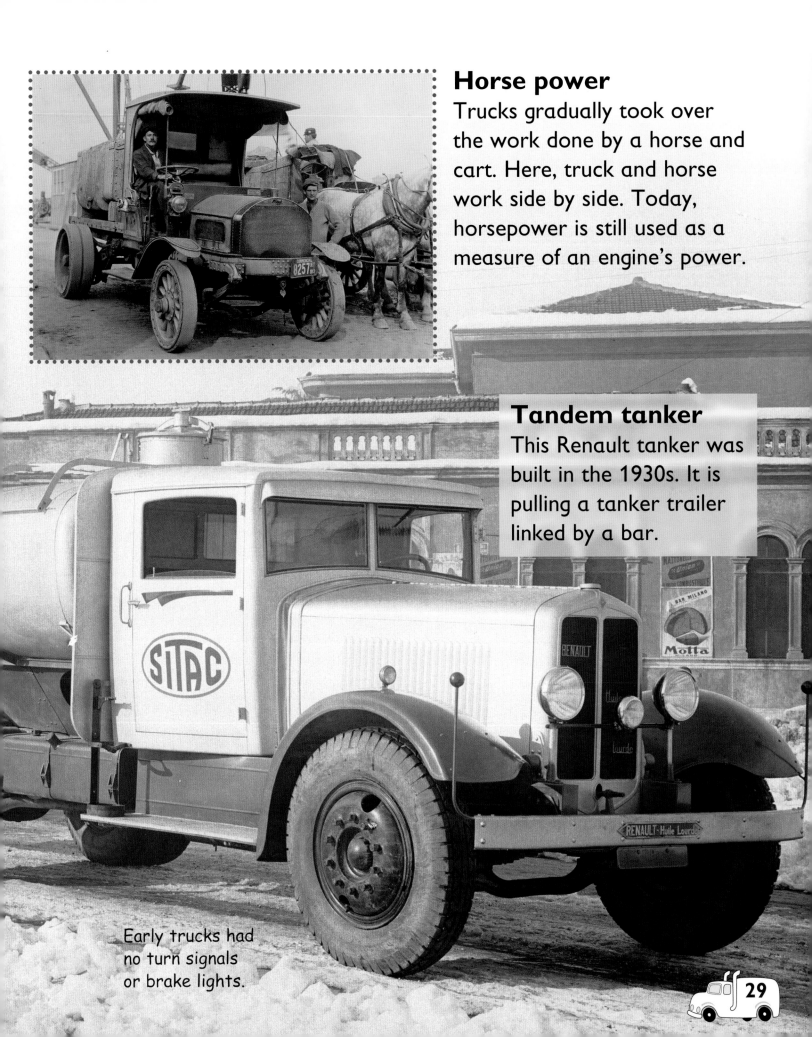

Horse power

Trucks gradually took over the work done by a horse and cart. Here, truck and horse work side by side. Today, horsepower is still used as a measure of an engine's power.

Tandem tanker

This Renault tanker was built in the 1930s. It is pulling a tanker trailer linked by a bar.

Early trucks had no turn signals or brake lights.

Picture gallery

Articulated truck

Articulated trucks can pull all kinds of different trailers. This one is hauling a curtainsider.

Tanker

The body of a tanker is very strong. It is made of two layers of metal to stop it from splitting open in a crash.

Car transporter

The decks of the car transporter tilt up to allow more cars to fit into the available space.

Customized truck

Thousands of dollars may be spent on decorating and equipping fancy trucks like this one.

Race truck

The driver needs a helmet, gloves, and a fireproof suit before he can race this truck on the track.

Logging truck

This logging truck has
a built-in crane to load
and unload the
heavy logs.

Snowplow

The curved blade on
the front of the snow
plow pushes snow
out of the way.

Road train

A road train is too long to
go into a city. It is loaded
and unloaded at special
road-train stations.

Giant dump truck

The driver of this giant
dump truck has to climb a
ladder to reach the cab high
above the ground.

Monster truck

The huge tires on the
monster truck help it
crush cars. The truck's
body is very strong.

Glossary

Articulated truck a truck made of two parts that can bend at the point where they join.

Axle a metal cylinder underneath a truck that connects a set of wheels.

Cab the front part of the truck where the driver sits.

Concept truck a special truck built to try out new ideas.

Customized truck a specially decorated truck with shiny metal finishes.

Diesel an oily fuel burned in an engine.

Dragster a truck that races over a short distance against the clock.

Engine a machine that burns fuel to make a vehicle work.

Exhaust waste gases from the engine that pass out through the exhaust pipe.

Fifth wheel a metal swiveling device that connects the trailer to the tractor unit.

Horsepower a measure of an engine's power. It was based on comparison with a horse.

Tractor unit the front part of an articulated truck containing the driver's cab, driving wheels, and the engine.

Trailer a load carrier that links onto the tractor unit to form an articulated truck.

Tire a rubber and metal ring inflated with air that fits around a wheel.

Index

Tractor unit

Acknowledgments

Dorling Kindersley would like to thank:
Truck & Driver magazine for help with pictures;
and Sarah Mills for picture library services.

Picture credits:

The publisher would like to thank the following for their kind permission to reproduce their photographs:

Abbreviations key: t=top, b=bottom, r=right, l=left, c=center, a=above, f=far

1: Sporting Pictures (UK) Ltd: Steve Perkins/Sport the Library (c). 2-3: Dan Boman/Scania. 4: Alvey and Towers (cl). 4-5: Volvo Truck Images are supplied by the courtesy of Volvo Truck Corporation. 5: Volvo Truck Images are supplied by the courtesy of Volvo Truck Corporation. (tr). 6: Photolibrary.com: Diaphor La Phototheque (tr). 7: Corbis: Phil Schermeister (tl). 8-9: Zefa Visual Media: Ed Gifford/Masterfile. 9: Corbis: Richard T. Nowitz (bl); Getty Images: Photographer's Choice (tr). 10: Komatsu (tcl). 10-11: Zefa Visual Media: Albert Normandin/Masterfile. 12: Corbis: Michael S. Yamashita (cl). 12-13: Photolibrary.com: Resnick Seth. 14: Corbis: Dewitt Jones (cl); 14-15: Corbis: Kevin Fleming. 15: Zefa Visual Media: Lloyd Sutton/Masterfile (tl). 16: Newspix Archive/Nationwide News: Dusko Maic (cl). 16-17: Australian Picture Library: Nick Rains. 17: Alamy Images: Gondwana Photo Art (br); Corbis: L. Clarke (br). 19: Sporting Pictures (UK) Ltd: (tl). 20: Hank's Truck Pictures (cl). 20-21: Photolibrary.com: Jon Arnold Images. 21: Alvey and Towers: Simon Everett (cfr). 22: Sporting Pictures (UK) Ltd: Paul Webb (tr). 22-23: Action Plus: Doug Murray. 24: Volvo Truck Images are supplied by the courtesy of Volvo Truck Corporation (cl). 24-25: Renault Trucks. 26: Corbis: Neville Elder (cl). 26-27: Action Plus: Neale Haynes. 27: Eric Stern (tr). 28: Hank's Truck Pictures (cb). 28-29: Corbis: Negri, Brescia. 29: Niels Janson (tl). 30: Hank's Truck Pictures (bc). 31: Corbis: Bennett Dean; Eye Ubiquitous (tr); Jonas Nordin (tl); Scania (Great Britain) Limited (tc). 32: Photo courtesy of Kenworth Truck Company (cbl).

All other images © Dorling Kindersley
For further information see: www.dkimages.com